What I Be, is a visual and musical journey about self acceptance.
It's okay to be just who you are and strive to be the best you can be,
by embodying the most inspiring characteristics of nature. Be as radiant as the sun,
as healing as the rain or as generous as a tree.

This story first appeared as a song on my album "Everyone Deserves Music"
and has been adapted in this book as a life affirming tale
for children of all ages, shapes and cultures.

The CD contains a hip hop and African musical collage of the story
featuring the voices of me, my son Adé Franti-Rye, and our friend,
Youssoupha Sidibe singing in his home language
of Wolof and playing the Kora (Senegalese harp).

I am sure you will find the music as enjoyable to listen to as the
wonderfully whimsical illustrations of Ben Hodson.

Enjoy, Michael Franti

For Adé and Cappy.
Be who you want to be.
- Michael Franti

To May, my soul sister,
and to all the children of the world.
- Ben Hodson

Published by
Stay Human Books
2180 Bryant St. Ste. 206, San Francisco, CA 94110
www.whatibe.org

ISBN 978-1-4243-3871-9
Library of Congress Control Number: 2007928095

Book and Type Design by Carla Swanson
Produced by Dante Orazzi, CreativeBeans.com
CD Sound Engineering by J Bowman

Printed in the U.S.A. on Elemental Chlorine-Free (ECF), Sustainably Harvested/Recycled Stock
with Environmentally Friendly Soy Ink

What I Be

By Michael Franti
Illustrations By Ben Hodson

Music By Michael Franti, Youssoupha Sidibe and Adé Franti-Rye

If I could be the sun,

I'd radiate like Africa and smile upon the world,
like intergalactic love laughter.

If I were the rains,

I'd wash away the whole world's pain

and bring the gift of cool

like ice cream trucks on sunny days

If I was the earth

I'd be like mountains, bountiful

and if I were the sky so high,

I'd be like wind, invincible!

If I could be a seed,
I would give birth to redwood trees

and if I were the trees,
I'd generate the freshest air to breathe

If I could be the leaves,
    like jade I would stay evergreen

and spread my limbs out wide...
and pull love so close to me

If I could be the roots,
I would dig deep
like ancestry

If I were the fruits,
you'd make the sweetest
cherry pie from me

If I could be the night,
my moon would replace all electric lights

and magic music would transmit from outer space on satellites

If I were the ocean

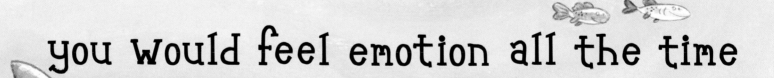
you would feel emotion all the time

and if I were the words,

cat
frog
arrow

then everything that everybody said
would rhyme

hat

dog

sombrero

If I could be you

and you could be me

then I could walk a mile in your shoes...

and you could walk a mile in my bare feet

What I be, is what I be.

Tell your own story.

If I could be _____

_____

I would _____

_____